A British soldier shields his eyes from the sun in the commander's cupola of Pz.Kpfw.III Ausf.J, tactical number '403' from Pz.Rgt.5 of 21.Panzer-Division. Charring on the hull side and turret escape hatch indicates that the tank was hit in the lower hull side and caught fire. The tracks attached to the driver's front plate were a unit modification, as was the 'Jerrycan' rack at the back, but the crew added the sandbags. Tow cables are attached to the front tow points, probably from a failed recovery attempt. **L.Archer**

"German tank Tunis 7/43 Henry Eckart, Maine" says the caption on this photo from a veteran of the US 1972nd Ordnance Depot Company. The surroundings look like Tebourba in Tunisia which fell to the Allies in May 1943. This Pz.Kpfw.III Ausf.M (note the exhaust pipe coming out of the back of the engine compartment which should have a muffler attached) has been carefully stripped of its wheels and tracks. The bent gun barrel is a very unusual sight.

L.Archer

Another Pz.Kpfw.III Ausf.M, this one substituting its Maybach HL 120 TRM engine for a GI. With large sections of the armour cut away we can see some interesting details, such as the dark colour of the engine bay, radiators and flaps for sealing the engine compartment next to the exhaust pipes. The exhaust muffler would have been bolted to the long bracket in the rear wall. An armour-piercing projectile sits atop the engine side-wall, barely noticeable among the wreckage.

L.Archer

More Panzer wreckage in Tebourba, this one a Pz.Kpfw.III Ausf.J. It has been stripped of all useful parts leaving us with an excellent view of the various mounting points and brackets on the side of the 'Wanne' and missing 'Vorpanzer' from the driver's front plate, only the spacers remaining. Despite the worn paintwork, a faint tactical number of '511' can just be seen on the turret side.

L.Archer

Another stripped Pz.Kpfw.III from the same veteran as the previous pages. Anything that could be reused to keep other tanks in the fight was removed: roadwheels, idler, tracks, gun. The tank has an unusual set of features in that the hull has an escape hatch but the 'Nebelkerzen-Wurfgerät' (smoke dischargers) entered production in September 1942, which suggests an Ausf.L or N. At least four armour-piercing rounds have penetrated the side; one in the lower hull, two in the upper hull and another that hit the junction of the upper hull and roof.

L.Archer

A fire in the engine compartment has charred the rear-end, weakened the torsion bar suspension, blown off the turret hatches and blackened the interior of this gr.Pz.Bef.Wg. Ausf.H. The main gun was a dummy and is shown broken, the only armament being an MG34 in a ball mount and the crew's three machine pistols. The purpose of the 'frame' assembly around the commander's cupola is not known. On the subject of frames; the 'Rahmenantenne' (frame antenna) has become a casualty of the fire, and a small section of this is lying on the engine deck. Markings are from the II Abteilung of a Panzer-Regiment, possibly Pz.Rgt.8, 15.Panzer-Division.

L.Archer

A shot-up gr.Pz.Bef.Wg. Ausf.H at a collection point near El Alamein, probably El Daba. With much of the turret front gone, we can see the ball mount for the MG34 on the left and aperture for vision port on the right. A number of rounds have penetrated the driver's visor, front plate and turret front, while the 30mm 'Ersatz Panzerung', usually bolted to the bow, has come away, leaving just the mounting bolts. The large white outlined 'Balkenkreuz' would have made an excellent aiming point for Allied gunners. **USAHEC**

Two shots of tank '115', a Pz.Kpfw.III Ausf.H, from Pz.Rgt.8, 15.Panzer-Division captured in Libya in 1941. The significance of the number '623' next to the driver's side vision port is unknown and does not fit with chassis numbers for the Ausf.H. The Pz.Kpfw.IIIs from Pz.Rgt.8 were fitted with steel brackets to hold fuel and water 'Jerrycans' on the trackguard next to the radio operator's position and across the top of the turret. The latter is missing here, just two small metal brackets survive. The bow armour shows the ghostly outline where spare tracks were once carried.

2x NARA

A New Zealand officer looks at the destruction caused by a direct hit from a 25 pounder during the El Alamein campaign and photographed on 15 September 1942. The superstructure of this Pz.Kpfw.III, complete with turret, was blasted from the hull leaving the armour over the transmission to support it. A barely readable 'Fahrgestellnummer' has been painted on the driver's visor which appears to start with '663'. If correct, it would make the tank an Ausf.H assembled by MIAG. The remains of spare track brackets on the driver's front plate and side bracket of a stowage frame at the back of the vehicle suggest that it belonged to Pz.Rgt.5.

ATL

The battle-weary Australian officer in the foreground looks as if he captured this Pz.Kpfw. III Ausf.J 5cm Kw.K L/60 single-handed. At least two anti-tank rounds have penetrated the turret: through the 'Vorpanzer' in front of the gunner and at the junction of the turret front and gun mount (next to the officer's head). The 20mm thick 'Vorpanzer' has come away from the driver's front plate, leaving only its welded mounts. A number starting 'L47' is visible between the radio operator's MG and bottom of the mantlet; this is from a truck in the background and not related to the tank.

2x L.Archer

Pz.Kpfw.III Ausf.J
Pz.Rgt.8, 15.Panzer-Division
No location
No date

Three photos taken by New Zealanders of tank '701', a Pz.Kpfw. III Ausf.J 5cm Kw.K L/42, which suffered a devastating explosion in the engine compartment, possibly from demolition charges. The top of the 'Vorpanzer' on the turret front has been repaired with an armour patch, and battle scars are visible on the bow and driver's front plate, but the grenade (attached to the turret lifting hook) has somehow survived the blast. The outlined three digit tactical number and stowage rack at the back of the engine deck indicate that this tank was from Pz.Rgt.5.

3x J.Plowman

Pz.Rgt.8 concreted the turret and fighting compartment sides of at least one Pz.Kpfw. III, shown here at Belhamed, Libya in 1942. The concrete was applied over chickenwire, which looks to have been held in place with angle-iron at the top of the turret. Whether this field modification was to improve heat insulation or for extra ballistic protection is not known. In the photo at right, a soldier from 2nd New Division stares in amazement at the wreck.

2x NARA, 1x J.Plowman

'Fahrgestellnummer' '72502', an M.A.N. assembled Pz.Kpfw.III Ausf.J from Pz.Rgt.5, as photographed on the battlefield and lower left, after clearance to the weapons collection point at El Daba. The turret has slipped from the hull during its recovery.

3x USAHEC, 1x L.Archer

The 'Fahrgestellnummer' '72628' on the driver's visor tells us that this is a M.A.N. assembled Pz.Kpfw.III Ausf.J 5cm L/42. British anti-tank rounds have scarred the bow, driver's front plate and gun mantlet, but a hit to the drive sprocket has stopped the tank, breaking the track into the bargain. Spare tracks have been draped over the turret roof and the tank carries extra roadwheels on the trackguard.

L.Archer

The Germans left one of their s.Pz.Sp.Wg. (Fu) (Sd.Kfz.232) (8-rad) armoured cars in the barracks at Sollum, Egypt, January 1942. The insignia on the fender of the truck at left is that of 15.Panzer-Division, so it is assumed that the armoured car belonged to the same unit. It has 'Zusatzpanzer' (additional armour) fitted to the nose which was a retrofit modification introduced in 1940.

L.Archer

Three more views of the Sd.Kfz.232 from the previous page, but taken at Tel-el-Kabir in September 1942, more than 750 km away from Sollum. Did the British really transport this armoured car 750+ km to a collection point? Or was it used for evaluation? Or is one of the captions wrong? Some of the wheels are non-standard, the centre two having smaller than usual tyres as well. The sand coloured paint was carefully applied around the 'Balkenkreuz', and a name, possibly 'Gero V.Hohendorff' painted on the front (behind the British soldier in the upper left photo).

3x L.Archer

During the war, the British Army published a number of booklets showing how to operate enemy weapons, including one on the German 8-wheeled armoured cars. The following is from *'Learn to use Enemy Weapons, Folder 11',* dated June 1944.

General:
This vehicle has eight-wheel drive and eight-wheel steering. It can be driven in either direction by means of duplicate controls located at the front and rear. The vehicle can be driven in either direction from the front driver's position, but only backwards from the rear driver's position. Aside from the change direction controls, the operation of the vehicle is similar to that of any wheeled vehicle.

Filler Points:
The main petrol tank holds 24 galls. and is located under the fighting compartment floor. The filler cap is through a port in the floor. A reserve tank of 6½ galls. capacity is located at the near side and is reached through a port in the superstructure top plate. The main tank can be filled through the tank by turning the reserve tank tap to the right. After filling the main tank turn the valve to the left and fill the reserve tank.

The oil filler cap and dipstick are located on the off-side rear of the engine and are reached through the engine cover plate. Oil capacity is 5 galls. A valve located at the near side of the engine cuts out the oil cooler in case of blockage or damage to this compartment.

The radiator filler cap is located below the off-side engine hatch. Radiator capacity is 10 galls. Air is admitted to the radiators through adjustable grills in the top plate. These can be controlled by the driver.

Starting the Engine:
(a) Turn on the main petrol tap on the off-side engine compartment bulkhead.
(b) Prime the carburettor by means of the foot pump located on the fighting chamber floor.
(c) In cold weather pull out the starter carburettor control knob on the rear dashboard.
(d) Turn on the ignition by inserting the key. The warning light on starter button should light.
(e) Press the starter button located above the ignition key.
(f) Warm up the engine.

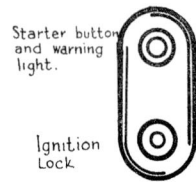
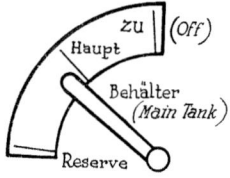

Controls:
Location of the forward controls is as shown.

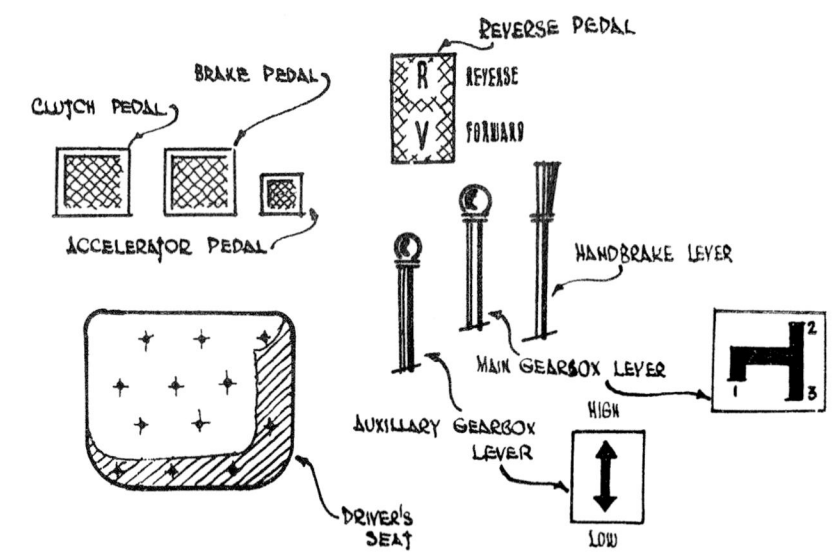

The reverse controls are located as shown

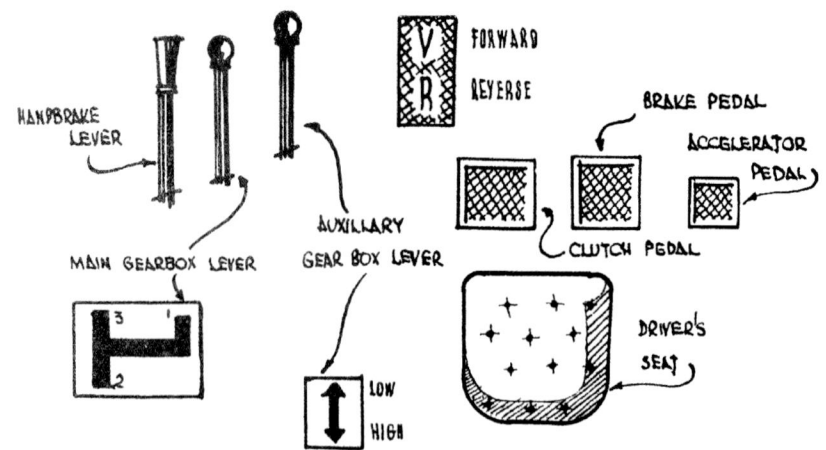

Driving:
To drive forward select forward gear with the pedal. Select first gear in high ratio and drive off as with a normal vehicle. When in forward drive, the rear steering is disconnected.
To drive backwards select reverse and the required gear, and drive off. Note that the position of the controls is reversed.

s.Pz.Sp.Wg. (Sd.Kfz 231) (8-rad), registration number WH-80628, was captured by the British in Libya and shown here after loading onto a Mack EXBX 18-ton tank transporter. The vehicle was subsequently transported to the UK for evaluation and then to Aberdeen Proving Ground in the USA. In the 1980's it was returned to Germany. **4x L.Archer**

70 miles west of El Daba, 1942. British soldiers pose with a s.Pz.Sp.Wg. (Fu) (Sd.Kfz.232) (8-rad) driven (or pushed) off a rocky outcrop. The vehicle is built on a 3.Serie GS Fahrgestell and has a wider turret, standard cast vision ports and at one point had been fitted with 'Zusatzpanzer' on the nose, which has since parted company. Another armoured car has been driven onto the 8-rad's back end, whose configuration of fenders, tyre-pattern and front-end point to a German 4-rad: Sd.Kfz.222, 223, 260 or 261.

L.Archer

Photographed in Egypt; a s.Pz.Sp.Wg. (Fu) (Sd.Kfz.232) (8-rad) based on a 2.Serie GS Fahrgestell, captured intact by the British. Like the vehicles shown previously, it has 'Zusatzpanzer' on the nose, although here we can see how far it protrudes from the bow armour; the 'Notek' driving lamp has been fitted on top of this. A spare leaf spring sits on the rear fender.

L.Archer

US forces captured a working s.P.S.W. (7·5cm) (Sd.Kfz.233) in Sbeitla, Tunisia on 20 March 1943. A simple field modification of two metal straps and thin sheet steel between the front and rear fenders has increased crew stowage, albeit at the risk of covering the contents in dirt.
NARA

And now with Allied stars. From the caption: *"This 16 wheeled German tank destroyer, equipped with a 75mm gun and dual controls for operating forward or backwards, was captured in battle with the 10.Panzer-Division in central Tunisia. The US Army star was painted on the weapon & it was put back into service against its former owners. Members of the new management are shown aboard here."* The date: 16 April 1943. Note how the German 'Balkenkreuz' has simply been painted over and the addition of sand-channels on the front fender. Martin Block tells me that this P.S.W. belonged to 1./Pz.Aufkl.Abt. 220 of 164.Leichte Afrika-Division, whose vehicles arrived in Tunisia in November 1942. **NARA**

No apologies for the poor quality photo. A GI poses with a s.P.S.W. (7·5cm) (Sd.Kfz.233) in Tunisia. It is based on a 3.Serie Fahrgestell and has exhausts introduced in late 1942, which had an extended pipe which doubled back up the muffler and output to the side, rather than downwards. The photo has had a hard life, and no markings are visible apart from a black 'Balkenkreuz' on the side. A schw.Pz.Späh-Zug (7·5 cm) each with six Sd.Kfz.233 was authorised in the of summer 1942 for the following units operating in Africa: Pz.Aufkl. Abt. 3, 33, 220 and 580, although it is unclear if all 24 vehicles arrived in Africa. Twelve Sd.Kfz.233 reached Tunisia on 16/11/42, a unit was quickly assembled and designated Pz.Späh-Kp. 'T'. Initially, this company served together with forces of Fallsch.Jg.Rgt. 5 and the Italian 'Superga' division. Thanks to Martin Block for this information.

L.Archer

A Pz.Fu.Wg. (Sd.Kfz.263) (8-rad) photographed by three veterans. The vehicle was built on a 3.Serie Fahrgestell and had cast visors, an armoured cowl over the rear air louvres and no internal reflected headlamps on the hull side. The legs that held its distinctive frame antenna have burnt through leaving just the telescoping radio mast projecting skyward. **Upper left:** With a British soldier. **Lower Left:** With the Aussies. **Upper right:** Much later after pillaging and three of the crew buried. Unfortunately, the photo quality is insufficient to see the names on the crosses.

3x L.Archer

Allied Armour in DAK service

The photographs on pages 26-32 are from a report written by Captain Wear of No. 7 Air Liaison Section, attached to No. 7 Squadron SAAF I quote the report and photo captions verbatim, the original photo captions are in grey italics, and my captions are in black.

Report on tanks destroyed by No.6 Squadron R.A.F. and No.7 Squadron S.A.A.F. during operations in October 1942.

To: Wing Commander R.Porteous, Commanding Officer No. 6 Squadron R.A.F.

Sir,

On November 12/13th, with Pilots of both the above Squadrons I visited the scene of operations in the Southern Sector to photograph and examine the tanks destroyed by the two Squadrons. Difficulties were encountered in reaching the operational area in view of the numerous minefields.

Six tanks on the feature Mungar Ralat (Square 8724) were examined and photographed. It is quite certain that there were many other tanks in the Southern Sector that had received attention from the Tank Busters but these could not be reached.

All the tanks examined and photographed were captured British machines and been quite positively put out of action by the Tank Busters. Shells and empty shell cases littered the area.

The tanks had been manned by German personnel and serious casualties must have been inflicted in the crews. One of the tanks which had received a direct hit in the petrol tank must have immediately burst into flames - none of the crew escaping.

Attached herewith are photographs of the tanks with comments on the damage inflicted.

Your obedient servant,

Capt. AA Wear
Royal Tank Regiment. No. 7 Air Liaison Section
Attached No. 7 Squadron S.A.A.F.

Allied Armour in DAK service

Opposite and this page: *Captured American 'Honey' map ref. 874242. Repainted German camouflage had been attacked frontally. Driver's visor must have been open. Driver probably killed. Shell passed through open visor through fighting chamber and into engine. Another hit on second driver's visor (closed). See close up. Complete penetration. Tank out of action for major repairs. Armour (40mm on front visor and 30mm on sides of hull).*

A British Stuart I, its only Germanic features being a large 'Balkenkreuz' painted on the side and a rear convoy lamp. **Opposite top:** With No. 7 Squadron SAAF pilot Jim Hollins. **Opposite bottom:** Penetration of the bow gunner's visor by aircraft cannon. The tank was knocked out by Lt. Aubry Rosholt, who was killed on 12 Febuary 1943.

2x UEA, 1x T.le Roux

Allied Armour in DAK service

This page and top two photos page 30: *Captured American 'Honey' map ref. 874243. 1 direct hit on petrol tank. (See close up). Tank completely burnt out. Hit through ration box and ricochet off front visor. Tank completely destroyed. Crew could not have escaped. Note gun covers still on.* This Stuart I remained in its British sand colour. The Germans have left the red square marking of a 'B' Squadron on the turret side and the War Department number T37908. This tank and the others up to page 32 belonged to Kampfstaffel des Ob. der Pz.Armee Afrika.

3x UEA

Beute-Panzer Mk.III
2./Kampfstaffel des OB der Panzer-Armee Afrika
Mungâr Ralât, Egypt
October 1942

Allied Armour in DAK service

Left and above: *Captured American 'Honey' (General Stuart) map ref. 875245. 4 hits. One hit penetrated hull and passed through transmission shaft killing driver. (See close up of inside of tank). 1 hit left track at rear. 1 hit in rear hull just below long range petrol tank. 1 hit in ration box. Hit also with machine gun fire. Tank permanently out of action.* **2x UEA**

Allied Armour in DAK service

Top: *Captured American 'Honey' map ref. 874244. Repainted German Camouflage. 1 hit in engine left side. 1 hit driving sprocket which damaged sprocket and broke track. Hit also on edge of visor.* **Above:** *Captured American 'Honey' (General Stuart) map ref. 874245. Track blown off Impossible to examine further as this tank is lying in the middle of a minefield.*

All the tanks had German markings although in most cases the British markings were still visible. Two of the machines had German wireless sets fitted. One tank had the Lap gun removed and metal plate welded. There seemed to be no other modifications.

2x UEA

Allied Armour in DAK service

Captured British Crusader map ref. 875243. 1 central hit on right side. Penetrated hull and entered fighting chamber. 1 hit penetrated engine. (Difficult to assess damage, petrol and oil leaking). 1 hit on left rear bogey and then into hull. Armour piercing .303 had split the track and broken some. (Tank out of action, could only be a runner again after major repairs). (30mm armour on sides of hull). In addition to the damage mentioned in the report, the auxiliary turret has been penetrated and the tank still carries the name 'Alice' on the bow armour from its service with the British.

2x UEA, 1x T.le Roux

The following is an account of the action at Mungar Ralat from *Panzer Tracts No. 19-2 Beute-Panzerkampfwagen*, reproduced here with the permission of Hilary Doyle.

On 24 October 1942 at 1800 a radio message sent from Kasta to AOK reported that:

1. At 0800, support Aufkl.Abt.33 with the Beutepanzer-Kompanie in the area 5 km south of Naqb Rala to counterattack against the enemy infantry attack supported by tanks. One Mark VI was knocked out.
2. Strafing aircraft attacked resulting in seven Beutepanzer being knocked out as total losses and five Beatepanzer damaged but repairable. Two killed and nine wounded.

A more detailed report of this action was recorded on 29 October 1942 as a Gefechtsbericht (combat report) for the 2./Kampfstaffel des OB der Panzer-Armee Afrika. as follows:

During the night of 23/24 October about midnight, the Kampstaffel was alerted by a telephone call from Aufkl.Abt.33. The enemy with about 70 vehicles had broken into the mine box southeast of Naqd el Khadim.

2.Kompanie was ordered to immediately strike toward them and if possible cut off the route over the Raqabet el Rala.

The Kompanie-Chef drove in the lead to gain contact with the Spähtrupp on the Naqd el Khadim. The Kompanie was brought up by Lt. Brenner.

From Naqd el Khadim one could spot about 15 to 20 vehicles including tanks at various locations to the southeast.

Shortly after the Kompanie arrived, a messenger from Aufkl.Abt.33 delivered an order to immediately start advancing along the telegraph line in order to cut off the enemy's return route at Munqar Ralat. At the same time Aufkl.Abt.33 was to advance from the east and join us on Munqar Ralat.

The point section started immediately. After briefing the commander, the Kompanie followed at a 500 meter interval and took up a combat formation after passing through the minefield gap. Enemy artillery fire struck as they passed through the second mine barrier.

Shortly thereafter anti-tank guns fired from Pt. 127. The loader for Uffz. Müller was wounded by an anti-tank rifle.

The Kompanie drove in a firing line in order to destroy the anti-tank gun and to take up a firefight with the advancing tanks. A section was sent to recon the southern slope.

An enemy tank was hit and set on fire during the firefight, the rest slowly pulled back.

Then the Kompanie split up. The left Zug advanced further up the telephone line. The right Zug circled to the south to go around Munqar Ralat and then rejoin the left platoon at the pass. During this action, the Chefwagen was knocked out by enemy tanks. A Spähtrupp on Pt. 77 spotted about 15 to 20 vehicles including 7 or 8 tanks in the area of Pass 116-135.

An attack by six strafing aircraft resulted in the Kompanie losing four Panzers, two killed, and 4 wounded. The Kompanie gathered in the area 1 kilometer northwest of Pt. 99 to reorganize and tend to the wounded.

Then the Kompanie took up position on Munqar Ralat and waited in the area as ordered for Aufkl.Abt.33 to arrive. The Kompanie received a radio message that, contrary to the original plan. Aufkl.Abt.33 hadn't started. The Kompanie was to wait further orders at their current position.

A new Spähtrupp was sent to the east south of Pt. 99. A short time later 12 strafing aircraft attacked and damaged or destroyed the rest of the Panzers.

After reporting to Aufkl.Abt.33, the Kompanie was ordered to leave a Panzer behind on guard and pull back to the mine barrier.

Above: Capt. Robert Robert Fenner of No. 7 Squadron, SAAF, photographed another captured Crusader. The German recognition manual for foreign tank types lists the tank as a 'Kreuzer Panzerkampfwagen Mk VI 746 (e)', which was often shortened Mark VI Beutepanzer.

T.le Roux

Possibly another of the Beute-Panzer Mk IIIs at Mungar Ralat, the flat barren landscape and lack of distinguishing features make a match difficult. The size, style and placement of the 'Balkenkreuz' on the hull side certainly look the same as the Mk IIIs on the previous pages. The frame in front of the commander's cupola was a British addition to make it easier for the commander to close the cupola hatch while standing, as were the blanked off sponson machine guns and stowage racks. This example has a broken track, part of which can be seen between the drive sprocket and first roadwheel.

L.Archer

Engineering; Roman and American. US forces recaptured this Beute-Panzer Mk III in Tunisia in 1943. In the background is a Roman aqueduct, probably the one at Zaghouan. The tank has a very fresh looking coat of paint and 'Balkenkreuz.'

NARA via D.Neeley

Allied Armour in DAK service

Allied Armour in DAK service

Unusually for a tank captured and re-used by the Germans this Valentine has just a single, albeit enormous, 'Balkenkreuz' on the turret side. Its British serial was T-27382, and apart from missing a run of tracks appears in good condition. The full German designation for the Valentine tank was 'Infanterie Panzerkampfwagen Mk III 749 (e).'

L.Archer

Allied Armour in DAK service

This Valentine was knocked out on the evening of 21 February 1943 after infiltrating positions occupied by the 2nd/5th Leicesters. The Bison emblem is that of Pz.Rgt.7, and next to the driver's visor is the 10.Panzer-Division insignia. Quite why the 'Balkenkreuze' have their colours reversed is yet to be established. The top photo was taken on 17 March, the bottom one on 15 March.

2x L.Archer

Allied Armour in DAK service

Among the lineup of damaged British Valentines is one bearing a neatly painted 'Balkenkreuz' which has been crossed out and 'BASE' daubed on the turret side. It carries the War Department number T-27271.

L.Archer

A much better view of T-27271, taken by RAF man Charles Taplin. In addition to the 'Balkenkreuz' (which once again someone has tried to obliterate), there is a large number '3' on the back of the turret and a very large and heavily worn 'Balkenkreuz' on the engine deck.

IWM

Allied Armour in DAK service

A captured M3 halftrack slowly sinks into a muddy road in Tunisia, 1943. The Germans have hastily painted rudimentary crosses on the vehicle, left the Allied star on the nose and applied the white cross on the door with the driver's side armour in the down position.

The halftrack looks like it has been stripped inside as well as out, but the M25 pedestal mount remains.

L.Archer

A very poor quality photo, but interesting nonetheless. A GI poses with an M3 halftrack an olive grove or orchard in Tunisia. The Allied star has been overpainted in what looks like a sand colour and a thin 'Balkenkreuz' painted onto this. For good measure, another has been painted to its left as a black outline. Two drive sprockets, from a Pz.Kpfw.III or IV poke their teeth above the armour behind the driver. Perhaps the halftrack was in use with the I-Staffel or Werkstatt of a Panzer Regiment? **L.Archer**

'Near Tunis', May 1943, and US photographers, accompanied by a civilian are at the Mediterranean sea. The M3 halftrack seems to carry the insignia of Fallschirmjäger Regiment 5, who obviously found the time to repaint it, complete with a sprayed camouflage pattern, add a licence plate and paint on clear oversized 'Balkenkreuze'. **L.Archer**

The caption reads: *"Damaged half track, an American vehicle after it had been recaptured from the Germans in Tunisia. It was captured by the Germans early in the fighting, German markings were painted on, and the machine was used to lead an axis counter-attack in the El Guettar section, where it was knocked out by the Yanks."* The 10.Panzer-Division used a number of these halftracks during the battle of El Guettar (from 23 March to 3 April 1943). Once again, an imperfect image - this one a wirephoto.

L.Archer

Opposite, this page and next page: Near the village of Boulaaba, northwest of Kasserine, 26 February 1943. GIs look over a Pz.Kpfw.IV Ausf.G knocked out by US artillery fire, one of 7 Panzers reported destroyed on 20 February. One shot entered the tank, exploded and blew up the stowed ammunition, completely demolishing the interior and engine. The 15.Panzer-Division insignia has been painted on the turret side (under the tracks on the turret) and turret stowage bin, and the Pz.Rgt.8 'Wolfsangel' insignia is on the stowage bin and rear plate. Both insignias would have been painted in red. The area under the tank has been dug out, possibly to give the crew cover from the artillery barrage. **2x NARA**

Just visible on the turret side is the number '7' and spade insignia used on Pz.Rgt.8's tanks in Tunisia. Close inspection of this clear and sharp photo reveals that there is a 'Fahrgestellnummer' painted low on the rear plate which reads '82897', making this a Krupp-Grusonwerke assembled tank. An interesting sidenote is that the spare tracks across the top of the turret have mud embedded in the track horns, so were once on a tank.

NARA

Believe it or not, these two photos show the same Pz.Kpfw.IV in 1949 which has unquestionably been used as a target. With the tracks gone from the turret roof, we are now afforded a better look at the markings on the turret side; the number '7', indicating the 7.Kompanie, 'spade' emblem and 15.Panzer-Division insignia.

2x OVH via D.Neely

Four shots of the same Pz.Kpfw.IV Ausf.G, the photo on this page possibly taken at the point of discovery by British forces, the others at the El Daba weapons collection point. With no markings pinning a unit ID is not easy, but the spare roadwheels in brackets either side of the engine compartment and brackets for spare tracks on the driver's front plate point to it being a Pz.Rgt.5 tank. The 'doubled-up' spare tracks on the bow are an unusual addition and over time these were reduced to one set of tracks and ultimately to none. The final photo has the addition of a 'crew' from the Polish 317 Kompanii Transportowej Pomocnicza Służba Kobiet (317 Transport Company Women's Auxiliary Service).

2x L.Archer, 1x J.Plowman, 1x PISM

5 November 1942, soldiers of the 51st Highland Division look over the remains of a Pz.Kpfw.IV Ausf.G from Pz.Rgt.8, 15.Panzer-Division that, according to the caption, had been blown up by Royal Engineers to prevent its recovery. The turret and upper hull offer a unique perspective and look like they have been opened with a can opener. **Inset photos:** From the same series; a large number '5' is visible on the turret side.

3x L.Archer, 1x TTM

New Zealanders inspect one of the new 'Mark IV Specials' (Pz.Kpfw.IV Ausf.G) knocked out near Sollum, Egypt and photographed in December 1942. The 'Fahrgestellnummer' '83018' has been handily painted onto the driver's visor making this a Vomag vehicle assembled in July 1942.

ATL

Pz.Kpfw.IV Ausf.G
8./Pz.Rgt.5, 21.Panzer-Division
Sollum, Egypt
December 1942

Three more shots of the same Pz.Kpfw.IV, showing its tactical number '843'. The hull ventilator behind the driver has been blown-off by an armour-piercing round. A powerful explosion, possibly a demolition charge, has flipped the cupola over and there is some blackening of the first and second roadwheels suggesting a fire or other penetration of the armour. A demolition charge has been set in the muzzle brake which has opened up like a bird's beak. The unit is 8./Pz.Rgt.5, 21.Panzer-Division.

3x L.Archer

It seems Pz.Rgt.8's Werkstatt Kompanie forgot something: a blown up Pz.Kpfw.IV Ausf.G, whose large three digit tactical number '412' and roadwheel bracket on the side of the engine deck are more typical of Pz.Rgt.5 than Pz.Rgt.8. The sign on the rear of the Sd.Anh.116 trailer reads *"Vorsicht beim Überholen Anhängerbreite 3m"* (caution when passing, width of trailer 3m). The opened box on its fender was a toolbox containing, among other things: 2 hand cranks, tractor-trailer signalling panel, grease gun, socket wrench and 2 shackles. Note the mix of British and German pattern tyres too. The top photo, a radio-photo, was taken on 10 December 1942.

2x L.Archer

British tankers give the 'V' for Victory sign on the remains of a Pz.Kpfw IV Ausf.F. The upturned fighting compartment shows usually unseen details such as the commander's seat and roof of the radio operator's position. Note the seat frame and ubiquitous bucket on the back end.

L. Archer

"Disabled enemy tank serves as an observation post for a NZ officer at the El Alamein front, Egypt" wrote photographer H. Paton on 29 August 1942. There are no return rollers or tracks on this Pz.Kpfw.IV Ausf.F, so it is entirely possible that the photo was set up and taken at a weapons collection point. The hole in the side of the fighting compartment is not a shell penetration, but the opening for the radio antenna, which could pivot to a horizontal position and supported in a wooden trough, which is missing here. The spare tracks bracketed to the driver's front plate and faint three digit tactical number are characteristics of a Pz.Rgt.5 tank. Note the armour patch on turret side.

ATL

A New Zealander and Pz.Kpfw.IV at a tank graveyard near El Alamein (probably El Daba). Interestingly, the tank has its 'Fahrgestellnummer' hurriedly painted in white on the bow armour: '82213', which makes this an Ausf.F assembled by Krupp-Grusonwerke. The spare roadwheel brackets at the side of the engine deck and spare track links bracketed to the driver's front plate point to this being a Pz.Rgt.5 tank.

J.Plowman

British tankers look over their adversary: a Pz.Kpfw.IV Ausf.F, after its destruction in Libya. The 'Werkzeugkasten' (toolboxes) have been removed from the vehicle, and one lies open between the driver's and radio operator's hatches. The tank carries the emblem of Pz.Rgt.8 and the 'Deutsches Afrika Korps' palm tree insignia on the driver's front plate. **L.Archer**

Desert Hunter: 7·62cm Pak(r) auf GW 38(t)

Death of a Panzerjäger. In September 1943, Hurricanes from No. 6 Squadron RAF test-fired rocket projectiles against armoured vehicles. One such vehicle was a captured Panzerjäger 38 für 7·62cm Pak 36 (Sd.Kfz.139). **Top Left and right:** The vehicle before the attack. **Lower left:** On fire after being hit by a salvo of 4 rockets. **Lower right:** Another salvo of 4 rockets on 3 September completely burnt the Panzerjäger out. **Opposite:** *"The vehicle on being hit immediately burst into flames which happens frequently since the cordite body of the rocket is still burning when the head penetrates - The vehicle was completely destroyed."* The rockets were fitted with 25lb AP warheads.

5x L.Archer

Desert Hunter: 7.62cm Pak(r) auf GW 38(t)

Desert Hunter: 7.62cm Pak(r) auf GW 38(t)

Above: Probably unrelated to the rocket projectile tests shown on the previous pages, a Hurricane IID tank buster makes a low-level pass over the carcass of a Panzerjäger 38 für 7·62cm Pak 36 (Sd.Kfz.139), Tunisia, May 1943. The wreck was undoubtedly a range target, and almost every part of the vehicle has been holed.

ATL

Left: Two British officers stand with a burnt-out and semi-naked Panzerjäger 38 für 7·62cm Pak 36 (Sd.Kfz.139). Most of the running gear has caught fire, and the gun no longer has its armoured shield.

A.Coles

Desert Hunter: 7.62cm Pak(r) auf GW 38(t)

Libya, 1942. The photo caption dryly says: "*Enemy self-propelled anti-tank gun. 6 pounder.*" Was it hit by a 6 pounder? Or was this an attempt at identifying the Panzerjäger's gun? A shot to the side has smashed the armour plate, another has holed a roadwheel, and the track has broken, making it sag. In North Africa, these tank-hunters were issued to Pz.Jg.Abt.33 of 15.Panzer-Division and Pz.Jg.Abt.39 of 21.Panzer-Division. There is some evidence to suggest that some were issued to the Pz.Aufkl.Abt. of both divisions after OKH authorised a platoon of 3 self-propelled heavy anti-tank guns for each on 20 September 1942. The third unit was 1./Pz.Jg.Abt.90 of 10.Panzer-Division who took 9 Panzerjägers to Tunisia.

L.Archer

Desert Hunter: 7.62cm Pak(r) auf GW 38(t)

Reducing its high silhouette: this Panzerjäger 38 für 7·62cm Pak 36 (Sd.Kfz.139) has been dug in which would have made it a challenge to spot and hit, at least until the gun was fired and a giant cloud of sand disclosed its position. The vehicle has been hit in the rear and caught fire, burning the paint off the superstructure and swelling the 'Jerrycans' on the trackguard. In the background is a Pz.Kpfw.III Ausf.J, possibly from Pz.Rgt.5.

L.Archer

Desert Hunter: 7·62cm Pak(r) auf GW 38(t)

A New Zealand soldier graphically shows how tall the 7·62cm Pak(r) auf GW 38(t) was. At least two of the three Panzerjägers have had their guns spiked by blowing off their muzzle brakes. The two vehicles in the background, numbers 'II' and 'IV' are clearly from the same unit: Pz.Jg.Abt.33 of 15.Panzer-Division as denoted by the 'Wolfsangel' insignia and tactical sign for a self-propelled anti-tank company on the side of the superstructure. In the background is a Sd.Kfz.8 or 9.

J.Plowman

Right and far right: New Zealanders climb over a lineup of Panzerjäger 38 für 7·62cm Pak 36 (Sd.Kfz.139) at the El Daba collection point. In the background is a row of Lg.s.F.H.13 (Sfl.) auf Lorraine Schleppers shown in more detail on pages 84 and 85.

2x J.Plowman

Desert Hunter: 7·62cm Pak(r) auf GW 38(t)

A scene of vicious close quarter fighting involving a Sherman II, whose name ends 'EOUS', and two 7·62cm Pak(r) auf GW 38(t). While the Panzerjägers look like they were demolished by their crews, the Sherman has been holed next to the bow gunner's position.

3x USAHEC, 1x L.Archer

Sgt. Harry Sherwood of the US 6th General Hospital X-Ray section poses with a 7·62cm Pak(r) auf GW 38(t), its only markings a white outlined 'Balkenkreuz'. Next to him and in the foreground are rounds for the 7·62cm gun, at least one being a Pzgr.40. The photo was taken in Tunisia.

L.Archer

Desert Hunter: 7·62cm Pak(r) auf GW 38(t)

Desert Hunter: 7·62cm Pak(r) auf GW 38(t)

What looks like a mine strike on this 7·62cm Pak(r) auf GW 38(t) has blown away the first roadwheel and broken the track. The dark coloured marks partway down the gun barrel were made by the gun travel lock rubbing the camouflage paint away, which is shown here missing the end and covered with a camouflage net. The inside of the bow gunner's hatch was left the original 'Dunkelgrau' colour.

L.Archer

Above: A British soldier in the fighting compartment of a Panzerjäger whose backend has been destroyed by an explosion.
USAHEC

Below: A GI with the 1972nd Ordnance Truck Company photographed this 7·62cm Pak(r) auf GW 38(t) abandoned near Buerat, Libya during the German retreat in December 1942. Given the location, the vehicle probably belonged to Pz.Jg.Abt.33 of 15.Panzer-Division. **L.Archer**

Desert Hunter: 7·62cm Pak(r) auf GW 38(t)

Above: The self-propelled anti-tank unit tactical marking in front of the driver, with the number '1' means that this 7·62cm Pak(r) was in the 1.Kompanie of a Panzerjäger Abteilung and given the US soldier and terrain, it is likely that the vehicle was from 1./Pz.Jg.Abt.90 of 10.Panzer-Division. What looks like a camouflage pattern on the front is oil staining.
P.Schiller

Egypt, November 1942. A 7·62cm Pak(r) auf GW 38(t) is winched onto a British tank transporter. Chalked onto its side: *"Do not remove anything. Evacuate to base M.I.(10) 4 BW."* BW = base workshop. MI-10 was the War Office department responsible for weapons and technical analysis during World War II. **Inset:** Probably the same vehicle at the School of Tank Technology at Chertsey in 1943. The photo was taken by the late Major Peter Gudgin from MI-10. Preliminary Report No. 20, dated November 1943 gives the 'Fahrgestellnummer' as '1548.' **1x ATL, 1x P.Gudgin**

Desert Hunter: 7·62cm Pak(r) auf GW 38(t)

Desert Hunter: 7.62cm Pak(r) auf GW 38(t)

Desert Hunter: 7·62cm Pak(r) auf GW 38(t)

Opposite: A Panzerjäger photographed near Sidi Barrani, Egypt in November 1942. The vertical posts sticking up from the fighting compartment held up a tilt for protection from wet (and presumably sunny) weather. Just visible above the side armour is a Pzgr.39 round. **Inset:** Probably the best-known photo of this vehicle and taken by a US Airforce photographer. The oil stains, bent trackguard and marks on the side all match. **This page:** The same Panzerjäger. once again. A British soldier holds a Pzgr.39 round for the 7·62cm Pak 36(r). Note the Italian tank in the background.

2x L.Archer, 1x NARA

Desert Hunter: 7.62cm Pak(r) auf GW 38(t)

These three photos show the Panzerjäger from pages 72-73, which has sustained damage to the driver's compartment because the side visor is missing. The driver sat on the right side of all Pz.Kpfw.38(t) tanks and self-propelled guns until the introduction of the Jagdpanzer 38 in 1944. The gunner's and loader's seats could be swung outside the fighting compartment to increase space, as shown here. Given the location and date of the photos (near Sidi Barrani, November 1942), it is probable that the vehicle was destroyed during the German rearguard action after the Second Battle of El Alamein.

3x USAHEC

A GI leans against a 7·62cm Pak(r) auf GW 38(t), presumably in Tunisia. It looks as if the crew have positioned the vehicle for an ambush: under a tree, next to a large cactus and with long grass covering the front. One of the uprights for the tilt can be seen in the background, and it is badly bent - perhaps an indication of an explosion at the rear? The rectangular object on the driver's armour is a head-pad from one of the vision blocks.

USAHEC

Desert Hunter: 7·62cm Pak(r) auf GW 38(t)

Desert Hunter: 7.62cm Pak(r) auf GW 38(t)

Two shots of a stripped Panzerjäger 38(t) at a weapons collection point 'near El Alamein' - once again probably El Daba, 40 miles west. The top photo was taken in 1945 and shows that the white of the (oversized) 'Balkenkreuz' was painted first and the black middle added after, as the two are out of alignment. In the background is another vehicle (without its weapon) and Pz.Kpfw.III, number '515', from page 14.

2x L.Archer

Kasserine Pass, 24 February 1943. A massive explosion, possibly from a mine, has obliterated the front of this s.Zgkw. (Sd.Kfz.9), totally wrecking its chassis and tossing the engine to the side of the vehicle. According to the caption, the halftrack was loaded with fuel cans and could have been a maintenance vehicle. Unfortunately, the ensuing fire has consumed any markings.

2x NARA

What follows is an extraordinary set of photos that show the lifespan of a halftrack; from use, to capture, to reuse. Here the crew of a Sd.Kfz.251/10 Ausf.C from Schützen-Rgt.104, 21.Panzer-Division looks out for the enemy. There are some notable details here such as the wooden 'shuttering' on the sides of the fighting compartment, armoured shield for the rear-mounted machine gun and the flying bird insignia on the front.

AMC

Although most readers will concentrate on the unusual variant of Sd.Kfz.250 Ausf.A with 2·5cm Hotchkiss anti-tank gun (from Aufklärungs-Abteilung (mot.) 33, 15.Panzer-Division), the halftrack to its left is our Sd.Kfz.251/10 minus its Pak 36. Reference points are the crushed appearance of the fender on the driver's side and an indistinguishable marking below his side visor. **Inset:** Both Sd.Kfz.250's have an elephant's head insignia on the front, but the Hotchkiss armed version has the addition of a flamingo!

AMC

Now the Sd.Kfz.251/10 has been given a new life by the RAF, possibly No. 33 Squadron (the photo was taken by a serviceman in this unit). Everything is in place for a perfect match: licence plate, markings, crushed fender and rear MG shield. Apart from RAF roundels on the sides and air recognition stripe and roundel on the engine deck, the halftrack has no obvious modifications. With no supporting documentation, it is impossible to say if the vehicle was used in combat or just as a mode of transport.

IWM

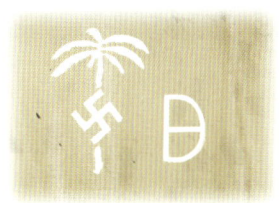

m.S.P.W. (3·7cm Pak) (Sd.Kfz.251/10)
ex Schützen-Regiment 104, 21.Panzer-Division
El Daba?, Egypt
1942

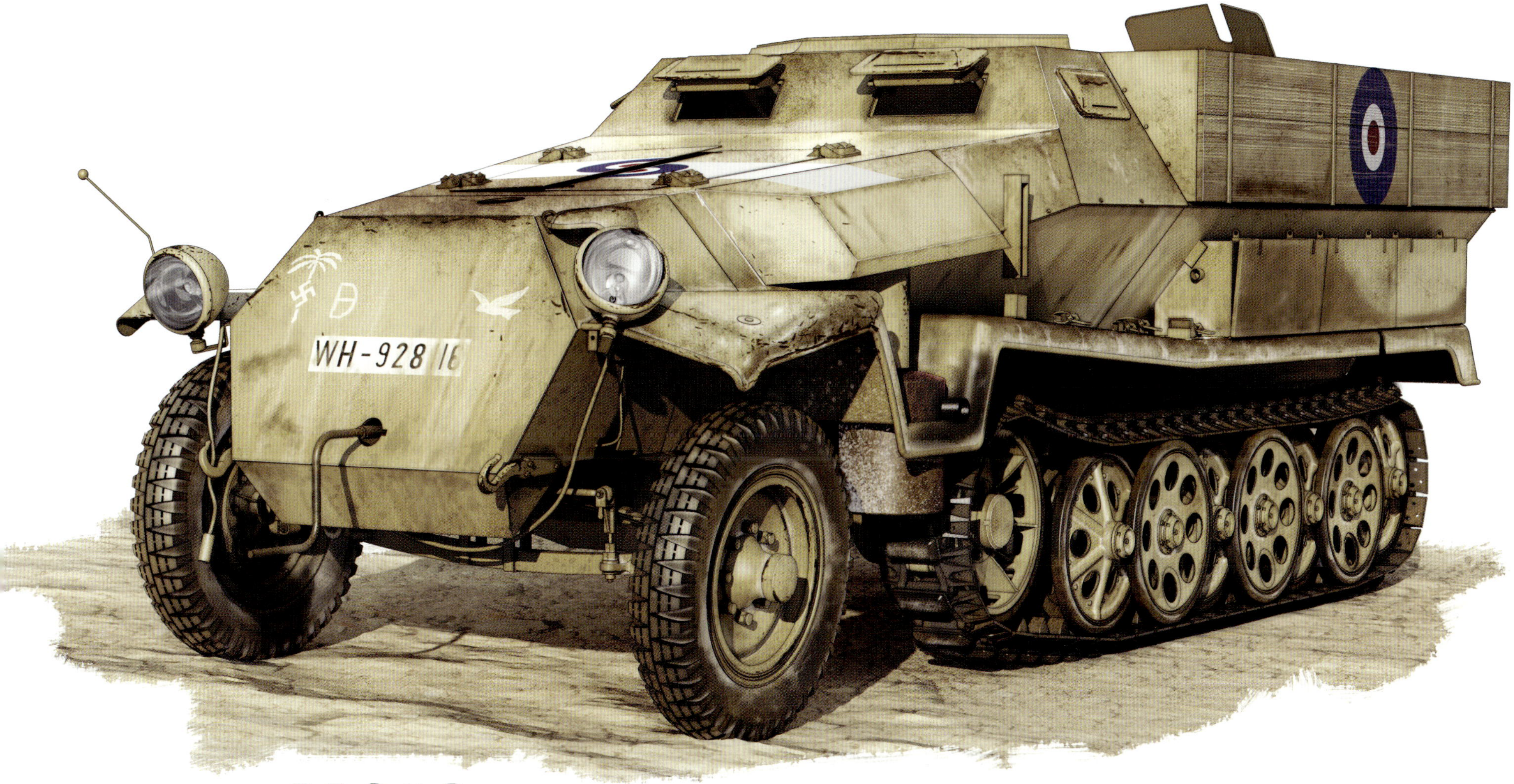

RODNA

Captioned as a *"German armoured car, Libya"*, a m.Kdo.Pz.Wg. (Sd.Kfz.251/6) Ausf.B. The large frame antenna sits atop the vehicle, its supporting legs having burnt away while inquisitive captors have left hatches open and liberated the front wheels. Markings are limited to a circular white emblem on the fender. The flat and featureless terrain perfectly illustrates how difficult it is to pin down a location for these photos.

L.Archer

Another halftrack, this one a m.Kr.Pz.Wg. (Sd.Kfz.251/8) Ausf.B and generically captioned as *"Knocked out Jerry vehicle."* The m.Kr.Pz.Wg. had no MG34, therefore no MG shield - just a pair of MP38's for its crew of two. One of the side stowage bins is missing, revealing the original 'Dunkelgrau' paintwork underneath, and it is interesting to note that the upper edge of the rear compartment is darker in colour where it was covered while being repainted in the sand colour. After this, the red cross insignia on its white background was applied.

L.Archer

A total of 23 Lg.s.F.H.13 (Sfl.) auf Lorraine Schlepper arrived in North Africa in August 1942 and were issued to Pz.Art.Rgt.33 of 15.Panzer-Division and Pz.Art.Rgt.155 of 21.Panzer-Division. Shown here is a selection of Pz.Art.Rgt.33 vehicles. The top photo shows a vehicle being recovered by British tankers. It was shipped to the UK for evaluation and, in June 1943, was the subject of Preliminary Technical Report No. 13 which stated that it had only 400 miles on the odometer. The lower left photo was taken at Sidi Barrani in May 1943 by a New Zealander, and the middle photo is the only one I have seen with a 15.Pz.Div insignia.

3x L.Archer, 1x J.Plowman

An s.F.H.13 Sfl minus idler and track photographed at a weapons collection point, possibly El Daba. The complete lack of markings indicates that this is probably a Pz.Art.Rgt.33 vehicle. In their June 1943 Preliminary Report, Major J.D. Barnes and D.M.Pearce noted that the colour of the example shipped back to the UK was *"light sand with slightly darker diagonal lines shaded over."*

L.Archer

The s.F.H.13 Sfls of Pz.Art.Rgt.155 can be distinguished by the large 'Balkenkreuz' on their superstructure and often carried unit markings front and back. A number of their vehicles received a field modification in the form of a wooden 'rail' around the top of the superstructure which was presumably to aid the crew's comfort when travelling as the 9mm thick armour would be uncomfortable to put a forearm on when travelling across the desert. Another field-mod was the addition of 'Jerrycan' racks fixed to the rear wall. These three photos were taken at El Daba, Egypt in 1943.

1x ATL, 1x J.Plowman, 1x L.Archer

Photos from New Zealand and Polish troops (from 317 Kompanii Transportowej Pomocniczą Służbę Kobiet) of the same lineup of s.F.H.13 Sfls at El Daba. The large white numbers painted onto the front of the superstructures are not German but British inventory numbers. The main photo was taken by New Zealand photographer George Kaye on 4 October 1943.

2x PISM, 2x ATL

Compared to the airmen of No. 318 Polish Fighter-Reconnaissance Squadron, the s.F.H.13 Sfl appears small, and the fighting compartment too cramped for three men to service the weapon. The vehicle, from Pz.Art.Rgt.155 was photographed at El Daba, but No. 318 Squadron was based at RAF Muqeibila and RAF Gaza between September and October 1943, both a very long way from El Daba. The number 'A242' painted onto the exhaust cover is not of German origin. The vehicle to the left has a 'Balkenkreuz' painted onto the lower driver's hatch.

PISM

Lg.s.FH.13 (Sfl.) auf Lorraine Schlepper
Pz.Art.Rgt.155, 21.Panzer-Division
El Daba, Egypt
October 1943

Soldiers of the Polish Independent Carpathian Brigade (Samodzielna Brygada Strzelców Karpackich) pose with a 4·7cm Pak(t) (Sfl.) auf Pz.Kpfw.I near Tobruk at the end of June 1941. No markings are visible, just a few 'kill rings' at the end of the gun barrel. **Inset:** Lt. Zarzeczny shows were an anti-tank round hit.

2x PISM

Another 4·7cm Pak(t) Sfl., this one with a British officer and missing the gun and half the fighting compartment armour. The vehicle is probably shown at a collection point or is among other wrecked AFVs because there are different patterns of track on the ground. Pz.Jg.Abt.605 was the only unit equipped with these tank hunters during the North African campaign. A photo of this Panzerjäger with its crew is shown in Nuts & Bolts 23, page 52.

L.Archer

Soldiers from the Queens Royal Regiment (West Surrey) look over or loot a knocked out kl.Pz.Fu.Wg. (Sd.Kfz.261) in this uncaptioned photo. The battle scars and flat tyres seem to indicate that it was attacked from this side. The Sd.Kfz.261 was equipped with a Fu 12 radio for long-range communication with headquarters and sported a folding 'Rahmenantenne' (frame antenna), which has split in two here.

SHC

Another kl.Pz.Fu.Wg. (Sd.Kfz.261), this one in better condition, and shown at a British weapons collection point. The vehicle is remarkably dark in colour and does not appear to have been repainted in theatre. The bracket on the side, behind the crew door, would have held the spare wheel, and the cylindrical object on the side of the engine compartment is one of two 'Filzbalg' - air pre-filters for use in hot climates.

L.Archer

A kl.Pz.Fu.Wg. (Sd.Kfz.261) captured in Tunisia in 1943 is looked at by a British officer. Identification is simple for this vehicle because it carries the divisional insignia of the 10.Panzer-Division and the tactical markings for the 'Stab' of a 'Kradschützen-Bataillon.' All is not what it first appears because the frame antenna has been added in the field: it is a different size, shape and configuration to the factory fitted antenna and is fixed to the vehicle on angle-iron brackets. Another field modification are the 'Jerrycan' racks fitted to the roof and rear fender. In the background is a Borgward assembled Zgkw. 8t HLm11.

L.Archer

Three views of a Pz.Kpfw.II Ausf.F. The large 'R' along with a tactical number '343' on the turret side indicate that it may have belonged to Pz.Rgt.8. A fire in the engine compartment has blistered the paint off the rear of the turret, and the triangular 'trough' for the antenna is missing. The 'Balkenkreuz' is unusually thick.

3x L.Archer

The caption for the lower left photo says *"Knocked out by ANZAC shell: A shell from a 6 pounder anti-tank gun, operated by New Zealanders, nearly ripped of the turret of this German light tank somewhere in the African Desert. The dead driver lies in front of the machine, covered with his camouflaged overcoat."* The location of the main photo, taken in December 1942, is El Daba airfield, in Egypt. Some notable details on this Pz.Kpfw.II Ausf.F are the 'Jerrycan' rack on the trackguard, leaf spring on the engine deck and details inside the upside-down turret.

2x L.Archer, 1x T.le Roux

A 15cm s.I.G.33B Sfl after capture by British forces. A total of 12 of these vehicles were manufactured, shipped to North Africa and issued equally to s.I.G.Kp. (mot S) 707 and 708, attached to 90.leichte Infanterie-Division. Their service lasted from January 1942 when they landed in Tripoli, to 2 December when the last 8 were reported as lost. This vehicle appears intact and is only missing the tools on the side of the fighting compartment. Unsurprisingly, the rack above the idler held 'Jerrycans'. **SHC**